I Like to Visit

The Museum

Jacqueline Laks Gorman

**Reading consultant: Susan Nations, M.Ed.,
author/literacy coach/consultant**

Please visit our web site at: www.earlyliteracy.cc
For a free color catalog describing Weekly Reader® Early Learning Library's list
of high-quality books, call 1-877-445-5824 (USA) or 1-800-387-3178 (Canada).
Weekly Reader® Early Learning Library's fax: (414) 336-0164.

Library of Congress Cataloging-in-Publication Data

Gorman, Jacqueline Laks, 1955–
    The museum / Jacqueline Laks Gorman.
      p. cm. — (I like to visit)
    Includes bibliographical references and index.
    ISBN 0-8368-4453-X (lib. bdg.)
    ISBN 0-8368-4460-2 (softcover)
    1. Museums—Juvenile literature. I. Title. II. Series.
    AM7.G56   2005
    069—dc22   2004057219

This edition first published in 2005 by
Weekly Reader® Early Learning Library
330 West Olive Street, Suite 100
Milwaukee, WI 53212 USA

Art direction: Tammy West
Editor: JoAnn Early Macken
Cover design and page layout: Kami Koenig
Picture research: Diane Laska-Swanke

Picture credits: Cover, pp. 5, 7, 9, 11, 13, 15, 17, 19, 21 Gregg Andersen

Printed in the United States of America

1 2 3 4 5 6 7 8 9 09 08 07 06 05

Note to Educators and Parents

Reading is such an exciting adventure for young children! They are beginning to integrate their oral language skills with written language. To encourage children along the path to early literacy, books must be colorful, engaging, and interesting; they should invite the young reader to explore both the print and the pictures.

I Like to Visit is a new series designed to help children read about familiar and exciting places. Each book explores a different place that kids like to visit and describes what a visitor can see and do there.

Each book is specially designed to support the young reader in the reading process. The familiar topics are appealing to young children and invite them to read — and re-read — again and again. The full-color photographs and enhanced text further support the student during the reading process.

In addition to serving as wonderful picture books in schools, libraries, homes, and other places where children learn to love reading, these books are specifically intended to be read within an instructional guided reading group. This small group setting allows beginning readers to work with a fluent adult model as they make meaning from the text. After children develop fluency with the text and content, the book can be read independently. Children and adults alike will find these books supportive, engaging, and fun!

— Susan Nations, M.Ed., author, literacy coach,
and consultant in literacy development

I like to visit the children's museum. I can learn about science there. I can learn about the stars. A group of stars is called a **constellation**.

I can learn about
how things work.
I can learn about
sound. Music is a
kind of sound.

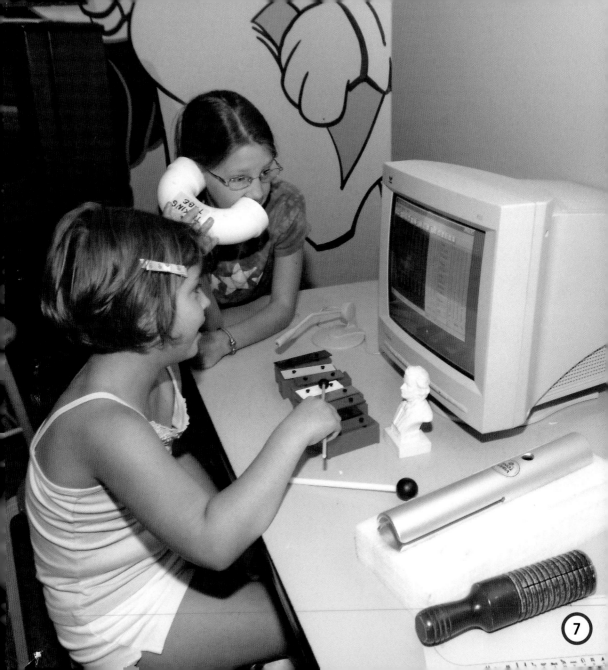

7

I can learn about my body at the museum. I can play with a model. I can fit the parts inside.

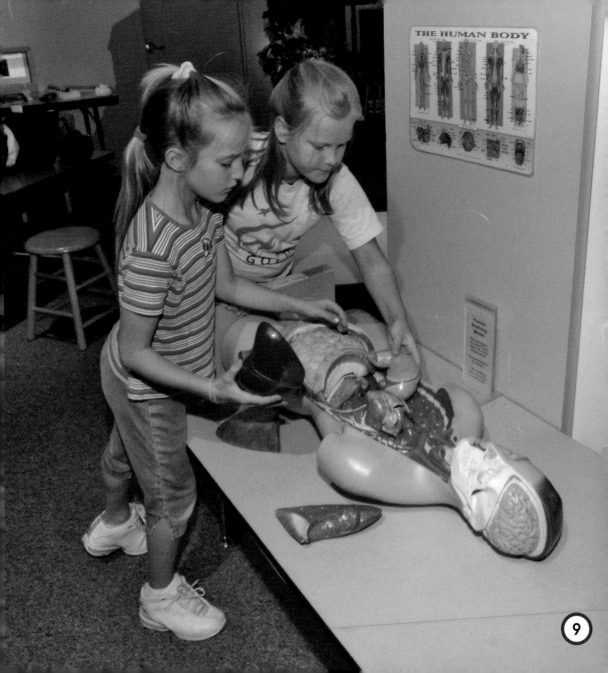

THE HUMAN BODY

9

I can learn about animals. I can learn where they live. Most lions live in Africa.

Bears in Africa?

Not today. But five million years ago a huge long-legged bear—*Agriotherium*—roamed on the savanna. The bear preyed on animals the size of a buffalo or larger.

I can find fossils at the museum. The fossils are from long ago. They are from plants and animals.

13

I can learn about space at the museum. I can learn about a ship that went into space.

DOCKING THE REAL
SPACE SHUTTLE

15

I can learn about rocks at the museum. I can see many kinds of rocks. I can even see rocks that came from space!

WHAT IS IT?
Find the picture that goes
with each rock.

WHAT IS IT?
hint: Find the
picture of rough,
light-colored lava.

WHAT IS IT?
hint: Find the picture of
rough, broken lava.

WHAT IS IT?
hint: Find the picture
of a lava "fountain"
(like fireworks).

from vol

I can see dinosaurs at the museum. I can see their footprints. I can see their bones, too.

Some dinosaurs were big and scary. Would you like to see a dinosaur?

21

Glossary

constellation — a group of stars that seems to form a picture

dinosaurs — reptiles that lived on Earth millions of years ago

fossils — remains or tracks of animals or plants that lived long ago

museum — a place where people can see interesting collections of things about science, art, or history

science — the study of nature and the world

For More Information

Books

Class Trip. Mercer Mayer (McGraw-Hill)

Let's Go to the Museum. Weekend Fun (series). Cate Foley (Children's Press)

The Museum. Field Trips (series). Stuart A. Kallen (Abdo & Daughters)

The Natural Science Museum. Field Trip! (series). Angela Leeper (Heinemann)

Web Sites

Children's Discovery Museum of San Jose
www.cdm.org/
Explore, play games, and learn

Index

About the Author

Jacqueline Laks Gorman is a writer and editor. She grew up in New York City and began her career working on encyclopedias and other reference books. Since then, she has worked on many different kinds of books and written several children's books. She lives with her husband, David, and children, Colin and Caitlin, in DeKalb, Illinois. They all like to visit many kinds of places.

24